# Observation Journal

## daily observation notes

"Scientific observation then has established that education is not what the teacher gives; education is a natural process spontaneously carried out by the human individual, and is acquired not by listening to words but by experiences upon the environment."

- Maria Montessori

| Date: | Weather: |
|---|---|
| Time: | Of note: |
| Room: | |

| Date: | Weather: |
|-------|----------|
| Time: | Of note: |
| Room: | |

| Date: | Weather: |
|-------|----------|
| Time: | Of note: |
| Room: | |

| Date: | Weather: |
|-------|----------|
| Time: | Of note: |
| Room: | |

| Date: | Weather: |
|---|---|
| Time: | Of note: |
| Room: | |

| Date: | Weather: |
|-------|----------|
| Time: | Of note: |
| Room: | |

| Date: | Weather: |
|-------|----------|
| Time: | Of note: |
| Room: | |

| Date: | Weather: |
|-------|----------|
| Time: | Of note: |
| Room: | |

| Date: | Weather: |
|-------|----------|
| Time: | Of note: |
| Room: | |

| Date: | Weather: |
|-------|----------|
| Time: | Of note: |
| Room: | |

| Date: | Weather: |
|-------|----------|
| Time: | Of note: |
| Room: | |

| Date: | Weather: |
|-------|----------|
| Time: | Of note: |
| Room: | |

| Date: | Weather: |
|-------|----------|
| Time: | Of note: |
| Room: | |

| Date: | Weather: |
|-------|----------|
| Time: | Of note: |
| Room: | |

| Date: | Weather: |
|-------|----------|
| Time: | Of note: |
| Room: | |

| Date: | Weather: |
|-------|----------|
| Time: | Of note: |
| Room: | |

| Date: | Weather: |
|-------|----------|
| Time: | Of note: |
| Room: | |

| Date: | Weather: |
|-------|----------|
| Time: | Of note: |
| Room: | |

| Date: | Weather: |
|---|---|
| Time: | Of note: |
| Room: | |

| Date: | Weather: |
|---|---|
| Time: | Of note: |
| Room: | |

| Date: | Weather: |
|-------|----------|
| Time: | Of note: |
| Room: | |

| Date: | Weather: |
|-------|----------|
| Time: | Of note: |
| Room: | |

| Date: | Weather: |
|-------|----------|
| Time: | Of note: |
| Room: | |

| Date: | Weather: |
|---|---|
| Time: | Of note: |
| Room: | |

| Date: | Weather: |
|---|---|
| Time: | Of note: |
| Room: | |

| Date: | Weather: |
|-------|----------|
| Time: | Of note: |
| Room: | |

| Date: | Weather: |
|---|---|
| Time: | Of note: |
| Room: | |

| Date: | Weather: |
|-------|----------|
| Time: | Of note: |
| Room: | |

| Date: | Weather: |
|-------|----------|
| Time: | Of note: |
| Room: | |

| Date: | Weather: |
|-------|----------|
| Time: | Of note: |
| Room: | |

| Date: | Weather: |
|-------|----------|
| Time: | Of note: |
| Room: | |

| Date: | Weather: |
|---|---|
| Time: | Of note: |
| Room: | |

| Date: | Weather: |
|-------|----------|
| Time: | Of note: |
| Room: | |

| Date: | Weather: |
|-------|----------|
| Time: | Of note: |
| Room: | |

| Date: | Weather: |
|-------|----------|
| Time: | Of note: |
| Room: | |

| Date: | Weather: |
|-------|----------|
| Time: | Of note: |
| Room: | |

| Date: | Weather: |
|-------|----------|
| Time: | Of note: |
| Room: | |

| Date: | Weather: |
|-------|----------|
| Time: | Of note: |
| Room: | |

| Date: | Weather: |
|-------|----------|
| Time: | Of note: |
| Room: | |

| Date: | Weather: |
|-------|----------|
| Time: | Of note: |
| Room: | |

| Date: | Weather: |
|-------|----------|
| Time: | Of note: |
| Room: | |

| Date: | Weather: |
|-------|----------|
| Time: | Of note: |
| Room: | |

| Date: | Weather: |
|-------|----------|
| Time: | Of note: |
| Room: | |

| Date: | Weather: |
|-------|----------|
| Time: | Of note: |
| Room: | |

| Date: | Weather: |
|---|---|
| Time: | Of note: |
| Room: | |

| Date: | Weather: |
|-------|----------|
| Time: | Of note: |
| Room: | |

| Date: | Weather: |
|-------|----------|
| Time: | Of note: |
| Room: | |

| Date: | Weather: |
|---|---|
| Time: | Of note: |
| Room: | |

| Date: | Weather: |
|-------|----------|
| Time: | Of note: |
| Room: | |

| Date: | Weather: |
|-------|----------|
| Time: | Of note: |
| Room: | |

| Date: | Weather: |
|---|---|
| Time: | Of note: |
| Room: | |

| Date: | Weather: |
|---|---|
| Time: | Of note: |
| Room: | |

| Date: | Weather: |
|-------|----------|
| Time: | Of note: |
| Room: | |

| Date: | Weather: |
|-------|----------|
| Time: | Of note: |
| Room: | |

| Date: | Weather: |
|-------|----------|
| Time: | Of note: |
| Room: | |

| Date: | Weather: |
|---|---|
| Time: | Of note: |
| Room: | |

| Date: | Weather: |
|-------|----------|
| Time: | Of note: |
| Room: | |